THE
HEALTHCARE
SURVIVAL
GUIDE™

THE HEALTHCARE SURVIVAL GUIDE™

COST-SAVING OPTIONS FOR THE SUDDENLY UNEMPLOYED
AND ANYONE ELSE WHO WANTS TO SAVE MONEY

Protect your Health • Protect your Wallet • Protect your Sanity

Martin B. Rosen AND **Abbie Leibowitz, M.D.**

Cofounders of Health Advocate, Inc.
The nation's leading independent healthcare advocacy company

Health Advocate Publishing, Inc., Plymouth Meeting, PA

Published by
Health Advocate Publishing, Inc.
Plymouth Meeting, PA

Publisher's Cataloging-in-Publication Data
Rosen, Martin B.

The healthcare survival guide : cost-saving options for the suddenly unemployed and anyone else who wants to save money / Martin B. Rosen [and] Abbie Leibowitz M.D. – Plymouth Meeting, PA : Health Advocate Pub., Inc., 2009.

   p. ; cm.

   ISBN: 978-0-9840696-0-6

   1. Unemployed—Medical care—United States. 2. Managed care plans (Medical care)—United States. 3. Unemployed—Life skills guides. I. Title. II. Leibowitz, Abbie.

HV688.U6 R67 2009
362.10425—dc22   2009928891

Project coordination by Jenkins Group, Inc.
www.BookPublishing.com

Printed in the United States of America
13 12 11 10 09 • 5 4 3 2 1

Preface

The title of our book,
The Healthcare Survival Guide
is no accident.

In the worst economic downturn since the Great Depression, millions of Americans have lost their jobs and their employer-paid health insurance. This has further swelled the ranks of the uninsured who are literally struggling to survive the complexities of our current healthcare system.

Simply put: Skyrocketing healthcare and insurance costs are increasingly placing healthcare services out of reach for more and more Americans. Despite the more than $2.3 trillion we spend annually for healthcare as a nation, a growing legion of individuals and their family members are forgoing needed medical care and medications, skipping routine checkups, neglecting vital preventive screenings and immunizations, and more. It is an especially dire struggle for those who suffer from pre-existing conditions, such as diabetes, heart disease, asthma, cancer, and other serious diseases.

The situation is bound to worsen as the formidable baby boomer population becomes eligible for Medicare—which itself has a range of limitations—and medical needs boost the costs even higher.

We've written this book to provide immediate information all in one place about affordable and, often, little-known healthcare resources. While we cannot provide all the answers, our goal is to provide Americans with information to help them safeguard their health *now*, when they need it most.

As we write this, our nation's leaders are debating reforming the healthcare system. While we cannot predict how this debate will conclude or what the future of healthcare reform will hold, it is clear that people will still need help to access resources and understand health insurance options. We believe that our experience helping millions of Americans navigate the healthcare system provides important insights that can help people today and in the future.

Our perspective is very straightforward. With the goal that healthcare becomes affordable, transparent, and accessible, we hope a book to help Americans "survive" the system will become unnecessary. And our mission to help them "thrive" within it will rise to even greater importance.

Acknowledgments

A book of this scope and urgency could not have been produced without a dedicated team approach.

Our editorial and research team headed by Marcia Holman and assisted by Sara Savage spent many hours to locate, research, and verify the very best and latest resources that individuals can really use now. Robert Boston created the book's unique, crisp, and lively design. Dawn Anderson and Jonathan Levine developed our companion website to provide updates to the book.

We would also like to acknowledge the critical feedback from colleagues who read various drafts to help make the book a better one.

This project would not have been possible without the support and encouragement of our company partners, Mike Cardillo, David Rocchino, Tom Masci, and Dan Messina, and the hundreds of men and women who work at our company serving the millions of Americans who use our service.

We want to also thank our families who were our biggest source of inspiration for this project and for their continued support of new and important challenges.

And finally, if those who read this book and visit our supporting website learn something that helps them receive the healthcare they need, all of the hard work that went into this project will have been more than worth the effort.

Martin Rosen   **Abbie Leibowitz, M.D.**

The Healthcare Survival Guide

Cost-Saving Options for the Suddenly Unemployed and Anyone Else Who Wants to Save Money

Lost your job and your health insurance?

Here are low-cost options to keep you afloat until your next job

When you lose a job and your employer-based health insurance, it can feel like being set adrift in a stormy sea without a compass. Safe harbor gone, it's hard to know where to find the resources to protect your health. Who will cover your doctor visits? How will you pay for medications? What if you get really sick? How will you handle a hospital bill?

This guide can provide a beacon to show you that options do exist, if you know where to look and how to use them.

As founders of the nation's leading independent healthcare advocacy company, which has helped millions of Americans through the healthcare maze, we've written this guide for anyone who has suddenly lost their employer-based health insurance. Here you will find practical, easy-to-read information for locating—and using—affordable healthcare options to secure the healthcare insurance and services so important to protecting your health—and your family's health—until your next job. **The book can also be an important resource for employers to help employees leaving their companies find healthcare options.**

How will you get coverage? We help steer you to the answer

Finding your way through health insurance options, the confusing lingo, the different stipulations, and, most important, the cost differences, can be a daunting, dizzying task.

Chances are, as an employee, you relied on your Human Resources department's benefit booklets to spell out coverage options. You checked a box, enrolled in a plan, and got coverage.

All that's changed. Now it's time to be an informed consumer and a savvy comparison shopper to hunt for and select the plan that fits your budget, your health, and your expectations.

We've done the legwork for you. We explain what you need to know to consider government, private, and individual health plans, and we provide the resources to help you access them quickly.

Of course, this guide is intended to provide general advice. It's not possible to anticipate every possibility, and there are important exceptions to some of the rules described in the guide. It is important to consult your personal advisors in any situation that involves your health or finances. This guide can provide you with the first steps.

How to get discounted—but quality—care?

You will discover how to negotiate fees with your doctor, uncover low-cost medical services in your community, learn ways to reduce hospital expenses, find low-cost or free medications, and more.

Finally, we've included a section on how to keep yourself healthy through regular exercise, a good diet, and other lifestyle measures. These strategies can help keep you out of the doctor's office and keep your expenses low.

For employers faced with the realities of the current economic climate, this guide can provide a relevant and important resource for their employees.

Keep in mind that as job losses continue and more people are seeking coverage options, new—and sometimes revised—information is emerging all the time. Websites and phone numbers may have changed from the time of publication. You may need to contact the specific organization that interests you to get updated information.

With this guide by your side, you'll have a solid lifeline and real help to find the healthcare resources you need—when you need them most.

The authors are cofounders of Health Advocate, Inc., which funded the publication of this book. The authors and the publishing company have received no funding from any other outside source or any other organization referenced in the book. A portion of the book sales will be donated to charity.

P.S. Communicate with us and stay updated

Our ultimate goal in creating our comprehensive guide and companion website is to help all Americans in need of healthcare resources become aware of the many options available to them.

We realize that healthcare information and resources are ever changing. And, as the healthcare reform proposals find their way into law, it is likely to impact some of the information provided in this book. This is why we have also created a website to provide important updates and which can also serve as a valuable meeting place. We hope that the website becomes a forum to share and exchange information, ideas, and suggestions.

Some of the most useful information comes from people on the front lines. Check in with us frequently, share your thoughts, and keep the dialogue going!

Email us at: **info@healthcaresurvivalguide.com**
Visit us at: **http://www.healthcaresurvivalguide.com**

A Lifeline to Healthcare Survival

Here's how this guide can help you chart your course to the healthcare you need.

Discover health advocacy

Get real help to navigate the maze.

Keep a watch on your bills

Are your doctor or hospital charges correct?

Consider COBRA

COBRA can be a temporary safety net. Only you can decide whether electing it is right for you.

Comparison-shop

Not all private health insurance plans are alike. Weigh them carefully.

Get drugs at a discount

You may not have to pay full price for your medications.

Take charge of your health

Eat better. Exercise more. Stop smoking. Reduce your level of stress.

Uncover cost-cutting strategies

Trim doctor fees, visit free clinics, and more.

Look into government-sponsored programs

Government-sponsored programs can be low-cost or even free. Find out whether you qualify.

All about COBRA

Is this safety net coverage right for you?

When you lose your job, the first healthcare option you are likely to hear about is COBRA, which stands for "Consolidated Omnibus Budget Reconciliation Act." COBRA generally applies to private-sector employers with 20 or more employees. If your former employer falls into that category and if you had employer-provided health coverage on the day before you terminated employment, your former employer must explain to you that you are entitled to elect temporary continuation of the same group coverage you had when you were employed.

At this printing, under the new COBRA legislation enacted in February 2009, the government will temporarily pay a portion of the premium. This could make COBRA coverage a more affordable option for you, at least temporarily. Here's the shorthand version of what you need to know.

What is COBRA?

COBRA provides temporary health insurance continuation rights to terminated employees for a period of 18 months. It offers terminated employees and eligible family members the opportunity to continue the coverage they received from their employers. Under new regulations, the government will pay up to 65 percent of your premium, if you qualify. You are responsible for the remaining amount due.

COBRA premiums can be lower than the cost of some private individual health plans, especially if you or a family member has a pre-existing condition. Additionally, since COBRA coverage is identical to the coverage offered by your employer, it may be easier for you to use.

Eligibility

Who is eligible

Employees and their spouses and dependent children are eligible for up to 18 months of COBRA coverage if:

- The employee worked for a company with 20 or more employees. (**Note** that state-required "mini-COBRA" may be available for individuals who were laid off from companies with fewer than 20 employees. For details about coverage and specific rules, visit your state's website homepage and search for "mini-COBRA" benefits.)

- The employee involuntarily or voluntarily lost their job (**except** for reasons of "gross misconduct").

- The employee's hours were reduced to the level at which they are no longer eligible for health benefits.

Who else may be eligible

- Retired employees and their spouses and dependent children may qualify.

- Any child born to or adopted by a covered individual qualifies as a COBRA beneficiary.

- Some independent contractors and others participating in group health plans may be eligible.

Who is not eligible

- Employees laid off by a company that closes or goes bankrupt are not eligible. However, those who become retirees after a company goes bankrupt are eligible for COBRA for one year after the bankruptcy filing.

- Employees whose employer ceases to offer any health benefit programs to its remaining active employees are not eligible.

- Employees who have lost a full-time position and changed to a part-time position are not eligible.

- Employees who are eligible for Medicare or the insurance plan of a new employer are not eligible.

The COBRA countdown:

Within 30 days of termination or benefit loss ...

Your employer must notify the health plan of your eligibility for continued coverage under COBRA.

If for some reason you do not receive the proper notification, contact your former employer's benefits department.

14 days after your notification ...

You will receive information about how to sign up, which includes your COBRA election notice. Generally, this means that you will receive notification within 44 days of your termination or loss of benefits. You may receive notification sooner (for example, at an exit interview).

60 days from notification to sign up ...

You must sign up for COBRA within 60 days or lose your eligibility.

When you sign up ...

You must make your first full premium payment by the due date noted on your election notice, typically within 45 days. If you have waited the full 60 days, this may include several months of "back" premiums. You must pay all of the back premiums to receive coverage.

Make your premium payments on time!

If you fail to make timely payments, you could lose your premium reduction and end up paying full price. You do have a 30-day "grace period" during which to pay the premiums.

You can elect COBRA for just one family member

It is possible to elect COBRA coverage for some family members, such as those with pre-existing conditions or who are pregnant, for example, and not others. You can then explore other coverage options for other family members.

Enhanced COBRA

Were you laid off between September 1, 2008, and December 31, 2009?

"The American Recovery and Reinvestment Act," passed by Congress in February 2009, is aimed at employees who:

- Lost their jobs between September 1, 2008, and December 31, 2009.

- Earned less than $145,000 if they file their taxes as an individual or $290,000 if they file jointly, in modified adjusted gross income in the tax year in which they will receive the subsidy.

Under this enhanced COBRA:

- The federal government pays 65 percent of premium costs for nine months of the 18-month period for which COBRA can be elected. Previously, the individual had to pay the entire premium.

- If you are unemployed but did not elect COBRA benefits within the 60-day period under the old rules, you now have another chance to be covered. Another 60-day election period begins immediately following your receipt of notification of the new COBRA rules from your employer.

- Under the new COBRA rules, employees who earned $125,000 to $145,000 ($250,000 to $290,000 if you file jointly) in adjusted gross income in the tax year may be eligible for a partial subsidy.

TAKE NOTE:
The COBRA subsidy of 65 percent of your premiums will apply for a full nine months, no matter what date during the eligibility period— September 1, 2008, to December 31, 2009—you became unemployed.

Eligible for the new COBRA subsidy but you've been paying the full price?

The Situation: You were laid off during the period of eligibility for the new COBRA coverage subsidy (September 1, 2008, to December 31, 2009), but before the new subsidy kicked in, you paid the higher 102 percent cost of coverage under the old COBRA rules. The 102 percent accounts for the total cost of continuing your employer-paid health insurance, plus a two-percent administrative fee charged to you by the government.

The Solution: You may be eligible for reimbursement for the overpayment. To find out, contact an Employee Benefits Security Administration Health Benefits Advisor at the U.S. Department of Labor at **1-866-444-EBSA (3272)**.

 Important Note

When you get COBRA coverage, it is an extension of the same health plan you received from your employer. This is important to know because if the health plan you are extending makes any benefit changes, the coverage you get through COBRA will change along with the health plan.

Disability can extend the 18-month period of continuation coverage

To qualify for additional months of COBRA continuation coverage due to a disability, the qualified beneficiary must:

- Obtain a ruling from the Social Security Administration that the beneficiary became disabled within the first 60 days of COBRA continuation coverage.

- Send the plan a copy of the Social Security ruling letter within 60 days of your receipt of it, but before the expiration of the 18-month period of COBRA coverage.

If these requirements are met, you and your entire family qualify for an additional 11 months of COBRA continuation coverage. However, the plan can charge 150 percent of the premium cost for the extended period of coverage.

Special Note to Retirees

It is important to know that if you qualify for retiree health benefits, you usually have just one chance during the standard 60-day election period to choose between those benefits and COBRA coverage. In addition, if you became eligible for Medicare less than 18 months before being laid off and you or your beneficiaries lose coverage as a result, you can enroll in Medicare for yourself and still get COBRA continuation coverage for your spouse and dependent children for up to 36 months.

COBRA Pros and Cons

COBRA is not necessarily the right choice for everyone.

Pro: If you opt for COBRA, you have time to shop around for other health coverage.

Pro: There are no pre-existing condition limitations on COBRA policies.

Pro: Being on COBRA counts as being continuously insured. This may be important as you look for other health insurance coverage later.

Con: Despite the enhanced COBRA subsidy, it can still be quite expensive.

Con: COBRA generally covers you for only 18 months.

Remember to check for updates

Programs, websites, and phone numbers can continually change.
We'll provide additional information and invite you to share important healthcare resources you've discovered too.

Go to **http://www.healthcaresurvivalguide.com**

COBRA Continuation Health Coverage:

Call the **Department of Labor's**
EFAST help line: **1-866-463-3278,** or visit
http://www.dol.gov/ebsa/faqs/faq_consumer_cobra.html

Employee Benefits Security Administration (EBSA)
Call toll-free to speak to a benefit advisor at
1-866-444-EBSA (3272)

**FIND OUT
MORE
RESOURCES
TO USE**

Government Programs

There's something here to fit everyone, no matter what your need, age, or income

When COBRA coverage runs out, or if you decide that it is not an affordable option for you, here are several government programs that offer less costly—or free—insurance coverage that may meet the needs of your family. These programs may be vital if you have children or if you or a family member fall into a specific group, such as having a chronic health condition.

Medicaid

This government program provides a range of medical benefits to low-income families, families receiving Temporary Assistance for Needy Families (TANF), and people drawing income support under Supplemental Security Income (SSI).

Who is eligible

- Pregnant women with limited incomes (married or single) and their children.
- Children and teenagers from limited-income families. Some states cover children up to age 21.
- Families on welfare with children under age 18.
- Those 65 and older with limited incomes and who are terminally ill, blind, or disabled.
- Certain people (pregnant women, children under 18, those over 65, and those who are blind or disabled) who have high medical bills they cannot afford.

Rules for basing eligibility on income vary from state to state.
Find your state Medicaid office by visiting the
National Association of State Medicaid Directors (NASMD)
at http://www.nasmd.org/links/state_medicaid_links.asp

CHIP for Children

The Children's Health Insurance Program (CHIP, formerly SCHIP) offers Medicaid benefits to children in families who earn too much to qualify for Medicaid but not enough to buy health insurance on their own.

For more information, visit **http://www.insurekidsnow.gov/states.asp**

Special considerations: when Medicaid is for all

If you have lost your healthcare insurance and have depleted your assets and you are hospitalized, you might become eligible for Medicaid.

State High-Risk Pools

Once COBRA benefits run out, about two-thirds of the states offer uninsured Americans with pre-existing conditions the opportunity to purchase healthcare coverage through state high-risk pools. These plans can be similar to catastrophic and high-deductible health plans. The drawbacks: they can be more expensive than the few private insurance plans that cover pre-existing conditions, and the waiting list is long. So sign up as early as possible.

For more information, visit the **National Association of State Comprehensive Health Insurance Plans** at **http://www.naschip.org**

National Breast and Cervical Cancer Early Detection Program

The Centers for Disease Control (CDC) offers this program to low-income, uninsured, and underserved women. It provides them with free or low-cost breast and cervical cancer screening and diagnostic services. Coverage includes clinical breast exams, mammograms, Pap tests, pelvic exams, treatment referrals, and diagnostic testing for abnormal results. Women ages 18 to 64 are eligible for the cervical cancer services. Women ages 40 to 64 are eligible for the breast cancer services.

For more information, visit **http://www.cdc.gov/cancer/nbccedp**

Free or low-cost health centers

The U.S. Health Resources and Services Administration (HRSA) sponsors this federal health center program designed for all uninsured and low-income Americans. It is composed of federally funded health centers that can be found in every state.

- Individuals who walk in and apply and are accepted pay what they can afford, based on income.
- Centers provide checkups for well patients, treatment for ill patients, and complete pregnancy care.
- Centers provide children's routine checkups and immunizations, family dental care, prescription drug needs, and mental health and substance-abuse care.

To find a health center in your area, visit
http://findahealthcenter.hrsa.gov

Federal Health Programs for Native Americans

The U.S. Department of Health and Human Services offers the "Indian Health Service" (IHS) for American Indians and Alaskan native tribes. Medical programs include specialty programs, medical support resources, and public health and wellness programs.

For more information, visit **http://www.ihs.gov**

Healthcare for Vets

Unemployed veterans and their dependents can enroll in the Veterans Affairs Medical Care Hardship program, which provides healthcare services, helps pay co-pays, and, in some cases, waives any existing healthcare debts.

For more information, visit
http://www.va.gov/healtheligibility/costs/Hardship.asp

Medicare Options

Medicare is an option for healthcare coverage for individuals ages 65 and older and certain disabled people at a younger age. In recent years, there have been some alternatives for the traditional Medicare coverage.

Traditional Medicare: Parts A and B

Traditional Medicare includes both Part A and Part B.

Part A (hospital insurance) covers inpatient hospital care and rehabilitation, nursing facilities, hospice, and home healthcare.

Part B (medical insurance) covers "necessary medical services," such as doctor visits, outpatient care, and preventive services.

Here are the basics:

• Those who contributed to Social Security will likely not pay anything for Part A.

• You must pay premiums for Part B. The government automatically deducts the Part B premium from your Social Security check if you have started collecting Social Security.

• Coverage is subject to various deductibles, coinsurance, co-pays, and certain limitations, such as first-day deductibles for your first day in the hospital.

• You can choose your own doctor and other providers.

• Coverage does not include prescription drugs.

• Medicare covers any pre-existing condition.

For information on eligibility, how to apply, and more, visit the government's **Social Security Administration** site at **http://www.ssa.gov/pgm/links_medicare.htm**

You can also visit **http://www.medicare.gov** or call **1-800-MEDICARE (1-800-633-4227)**

Medicare Advantage (also known as Medicare Part C)

This alternative to traditional Medicare is offered by many private insurance companies and includes hospital and medical insurance similar to that of Medicare Parts A and B. Medicare Advantage plans cover pre-existing conditions, such as diabetes and asthma, for example. If you join a Medicare Advantage plan, you may have lower out-of-pocket costs and broader coverage than traditional Medicare. Some Medicare Advantage plans even include prescription drug coverage.

Here are key features of Medicare Advantage plans:

• You are still responsible for paying the same premium as with traditional Medicare Part B.

• Depending on the Medicare Advantage plan you select, you might also have to pay additional premiums.

• Some of these plans also have out-of-pocket costs, including co-pays.

• Depending on the plan (e.g. HMO, PPO), you will have to use in-network providers and may need referrals for some medical services.

There are many different Medicare Advantage plans.

Medicare Advantage plans include health maintenance organization (HMO) plans, preferred provider organization (PPO) plans, and private fee-for-service (PFFS) plans. The least expensive and most common is a Medicare HMO. Medicare HMOs give you coverage similar to Medicare Parts A and B, but your care is limited to doctors within the HMO network.

To find Medicare Advantage coverage insurance, check with private insurance providers such as Aetna, CIGNA, Kaiser Permanente, AARP MedicareComplete, Humana, Blue Cross and Blue Shield, and others.

For general definitions of HMOs, PPOs and other plans, see **Comparison-Shop for Coverage.**

More Medicare Options

Medicare Part D

If you want drug coverage and you are enrolled in a traditional Medicare plan or a Medicare Advantage plan, you can choose to buy Medicare Part D, a supplemental plan offered through Medicare-approved private companies. Part D covers much of the cost of prescription drugs. There are different formularies and other limitations in these plans, so investigate your options carefully.

For more information on Medicare Part D, visit **http://www.medicare.gov** or call **1-800-MEDICARE (1-800-633-4227)**

Medigap: covers gaps left by Medicare coverage

Private insurance companies offer Medigap programs, also known as "Medicare Supplemental Insurance," which cover what traditional Medicare does not, such as co-pays, coinsurance, and deductibles. There are a number of different Medigap program options, from basic to comprehensive. Medigap policies expand your traditional coverage and also eliminate first-day deductibles for hospital stays. All companies are required to offer the same Medigap policies, but the cost of the policies can be different from company to company, so shop around.

To find Medigap coverage, check with private insurance providers such as Kaiser Permanente, Aetna, AARP MedicareComplete, and Blue Cross and Blue Shield.

Still unsure about the right program? Here are key contacts:

U.S. Uninsured Help Line: call **1-800-234-1317** to speak to a benefits representative

Foundation for Health Coverage Education (FHCE): http://www.coverageforall.org

Remember to check for updates

Programs, websites, and phone numbers can continually change. We'll provide additional information and invite you to share important healthcare resources you've discovered too.

Go to **http://www.healthcaresurvivalguide.com**

Comparison-Shop for Coverage

How to choose what you need, when you need it

Private health plans come in every shape and size, and only you can decide which one fits best. Making an informed decision depends on your budget and expectations, as well as your medical needs. A licensed insurance broker can review the costs, coverage, and plan limitations with you. Doing your own homework can also pay off.

Look beyond the premium price

- See what the plan does and does not cover.

- Some plans have annual or lifetime limits for particular services, or for what they will pay in total for care.

- Review the co-payments (the fixed amount you must pay) for doctor visits, emergency room care, outpatient services, and hospitalization.

- Check the deductibles—what you must pay before your plan pays.

- Keep in mind that a plan with a lower premium can mean that you will have to pay higher deductibles and co-pays when you need care.

- Take a look at the coinsurance arrangement. Find out how much of your medical coverage you will be required to pay. Some plans include a coinsurance cap that sets limits on your out-of-pocket expenses, but caps do not usually apply to non-covered services or for care provided out-of-network.

How far does the coverage stretch?

See whether the policy covers pre-existing health conditions, behavioral health, maternity care, preventive screenings, and regular checkups.
If pregnancy is in your near future, note that some individual health plans offer maternity coverage only when you buy an extra rider (or additional coverage).
Remember to find out about the waiting period before coverage starts.

What you need to know to get started

If you have a pre-existing condition, take heart ...

Under the Health Insurance Portability and Accountability Act (HIPAA), if you have a pre-existing condition and you were covered for at least a year up until your date of termination, you cannot be discriminated against for healthcare coverage. Your former employer is required to provide you with a "certificate of creditable coverage" that you can use to show your new plan that you have not had a 63-day gap in coverage.

Be sure to act quickly though, because your new insurer can deny coverage for pre-existing conditions if you have a gap in healthcare coverage greater than 63 days. If you go without health coverage for more than 63 days, you may lose some of HIPAA's protections for coverage of pre-existing conditions. Some states require that you have even more than 63 days of continuous coverage in order to be exempt from pre-existing condition limitations.

For more information about **HIPAA coverage,** visit **http://www.hhs.gov/ocr/hipaa**

Learn the lingo: words to know

Co-pay: The fixed amount you pay for doctor visits or when you receive medical services or medications.

Deductible: The total amount of out-of-pocket costs you have to pay before your insurance coverage begins.

Premium: Periodic payments required to keep your insurance policy in effect.

Coinsurance: The percentage of the charge that you pay for covered services. In most policies, there are annual limits to the amount of money you can pay for covered services.

Generic drugs: Generally less expensive versions of medications that are chemically the same as brand-name drugs.

Plans with Coinsurance

Health plans that feature coinsurance provisions are designed so that you and your insurance company split the cost of your covered healthcare services by a certain fixed percentage. Generally, your deductible must be met and you have to pay any co-pays before your insurance company pays anything. A common percentage split between the plan and the individual is 80/20, meaning the plan pays 80 percent and you pay 20 percent.

- In order for the insurance company to pay for a service, it must first determine the amount it considers to be a "reasonable and customary" charge for the service. Reasonable and customary charges are typically based on the average amount charged for the same service by other doctors or providers in your area.

- For an 80/20 cost share, the insurance company will pay 80 percent of the reasonable and customary amount, while you pay the remaining 20 percent.

- If you go to an out-of-network or non-contracted provider, you can be balance-billed for the difference between the amount the provider billed and the total amount that you and your plan paid for the care you received. When this happens, you are responsible for paying the difference.

- Typically, once you reach your out-of-pocket maximum, your insurance company will pay 100 percent of your covered healthcare costs as long as the care you need is provided by an in-network or contracted provider. Note that the amount billed for non-covered services or the amount balance-billed by non-contracted or out-of-network providers does not count toward your out-of-pocket maximum!

Special consideration if you have diabetes

If you are one of the 24 million Americans who have diabetes, your medical expenses are likely to be more than twice as high as for someone without the disease. So it pays to do research about the cost of treatment.

For a state-by-state estimate, visit **http://www.diabetes.org/ advocacy-and-legalresources/cost-of-diabetes.jsp**

25

Red Flags

To avoid surprises later on, read your health plan carefully. Be on the lookout for:

- **Coverage limits.** The plan's limits on coverage could leave you with big bills if you have a true health crisis.

- **Caps on care.** Look for any maximum limits on what the plan will pay for any service, including hospitalizations and doctor visits.

- **Missing parts.** Chances are that if the plan documents do not mention benefits such as treatment for certain conditions or prescription coverage, then it's not a benefit!

- **No mention of a maximum limit on out-of-pocket costs.** You could pay hundreds or even thousands of dollars if the plan has no limits on your out-of-pocket expenses. Better coverage should pay 100 percent for covered services from contracted or in-network providers once your out-of-pocket limit has been met.

- **Delays in coverage activation.** Look to see whether the plan has a waiting period before coverage begins or limits on coverage for pre-existing conditions. You may not be covered when you need it most.

- **Watch out for condition exclusions.** Some plans may specifically exclude coverage for heart disease, cancer, or pregnancy, for example.

Affordable can mean limited coverage

If you want a truly comprehensive plan, it should be "unlimited." Coverage should include hospitalization (inpatient and outpatient), ambulance, ER, all diagnostic tests, rehabilitation, physical therapy, mental health treatment, medications, and any medical equipment.

Health Plans: One size does not fit all

Understand the differences. Select the plan that is best for you.

HMO (Health Maintenance Organization)

HMO coverage requires you to go to participating network doctors, hospitals, and other healthcare providers.

PPO (Preferred Provider Organization)

PPOs offer two options: using participating in-network providers or going outside the network to nonparticipating providers.

POS (Point of Service)

POS plans combine some of the features found in HMOs and PPOs.

HDHP (High-Deductible Health Plans)

Also known as consumer-driven health plans (CDHPs)

HDHPs are generally like PPO plans that require you to meet an annual deductible before your insurance company pays anything.

Catastrophic Health Insurance

Catastrophic health insurance plans provide coverage for major medical and hospital costs, including surgery, hospital stays, intensive care, X-rays, and lab tests.

Hospital and Preventive Health Plans

Hospital and preventive healthcare plans can be found through major insurance companies and cover inpatient hospital stays and any hospital services rendered. These plans do not cover primary care services, but some include drug discounts.

Generally, members are required to obtain a referral from their primary care physician for all non-emergency care. Use of non-network providers will not be covered unless specifically authorized by the HMO. Coverage is typically comprehensive when using network providers, subject to various co-pay provisions.

You may be subject to a combination of co-pays, coinsurance, and deductibles, but the amount you have to pay will always be less if you get care in the network from participating providers. PPO plan benefits can vary more widely than HMO benefits do.

You can get care in the network from participating providers by obtaining referrals from your primary care physician when necessary, much like with an HMO. But members are also permitted to go directly to in- or out-of-network providers without obtaining a referral, subject to higher co-pays, deductibles, and coinsurance, as in a PPO plan.

HDHPs carry higher annual deductibles than other plans. These deductibles lead to lower premiums, and you may choose to use both in- and out-of-network providers, but staying in-network will save you money. HDHPs can be combined with various kinds of medical savings accounts (HSA, MSA, FSA, etc.).

These plans can take several forms. Some offer comprehensive coverage after a very large deductible ($10,000 or more for example) is met. Others, called "Major Medical" programs, pay a fixed amount for a particular service regardless of the provider's charge. These policies often have lifetime limits on how much they will pay.

Catastrophic health insurance plans are typically chosen by healthy young adults and older, healthy adults nearing Medicare eligibility who need coverage but cannot afford more comprehensive insurance.

Preventive care plans cover blood tests, immunizations, and screenings such as mammograms and prostate exams, and lab work.

These plans are targeted to those who don't want to pay for coverage they don't need, but who want insurance in the event of a major accident or illness.

When all you need is basic coverage, consider mini-medical/limited benefit plans

Mini-medical plans, also known as "limited benefit" plans, may be a good option if you are in good health but want just basic coverage, such as doctor's visits, lab work, X-rays, and prescription drugs. There are no deductibles or co-pays, and you have network provider choices that can save you money. In most cases, there are no waiting periods—except for pre-existing conditions.

However, these plans, offered by companies such as United Group, Allstate, and lesser-known providers, may be quite limited in terms of benefits. Some plans only cover four to 10 doctor visits a year. Premiums can be as low as $40 per month. Many mini-medical plans also have yearly coverage caps of $10,000 or less.

For a free mini-medical plan quote, visit **http://mini-medical-insurance.org**

What drugs does the plan cover?

Most prescription drug plans use a **formulary**, the list of covered drugs available at lower cost. Check to see whether your medications are on the plan's formulary. Look at the co-pay for each prescription and whether the plan has a limit on the amount it will pay. Remember that formulary lists may change each year.

Get a 90-day supply: If the plan offers a mail-order service, ask your doctor to write a prescription for a 90-day supply of your medications. This will save you money because you'll pay fewer co-pays.

Switch to generics: In most prescription drug plans, generic drugs are less expensive. Check with your doctor to see whether it is possible to switch to a generic version of your medication. If the medications are not on the plan's formulary, see whether your doctor thinks you could switch to a formulary medication instead.

For more information on lower-cost prescription medication, see **Best Ways to Get Drugs at a Discount (or Free!).**

Avoid Sticker Shock

Costs associated with the treatment of many common conditions and procedures can reach several thousands of dollars a year for prescription drugs, testing, and physician visits. And costs can climb to more than a quarter million dollars for the treatment of some cancers. Co-pays can vary widely, too. So make sure your plan meets your needs.

In top health?
Explore High-Deductible Health Plans (HDHPs)

If you are younger, in good health, and do not regularly use medical services, a higher-deductible/lower-monthly-premium plan, sometimes known as a consumer-driven health plan (CDHP), may be a good option. These plans generally offer a full range of services, including routine coverage for physical exams and preventive care provided by the doctor.

However, in return for their lower premium, you will be required to pay more out-of-pocket before coverage kicks in.

Job on the horizon?
Consider lower cost, short-term health insurance

Many private insurance providers offer low-cost coverage for one to six months for individuals and families, that can provide a safety net in the event of an unexpected illness or injury. These plans generally offer coverage for physician services related to illnesses, including surgery and outpatient and inpatient care.

However, the plans may offer limited or no coverage for pre-existing conditions, routine exams, maternity care, or preventive care, such as regular childhood wellness visits, and immunizations and dental care. So check the terms of coverage before you buy.

The wait for coverage is short, and you'll have the option of paying monthly premiums. These plans can also be used to provide "gap" coverage for older individuals who are nearing eligibility for Medicare.

If you're over 50 with a pre-existing condition

The AARP (American Association of Retired Persons) partners with Aetna and other major health insurance companies to offer a low cost Essential Premier Health Insurance plan. If you had coverage within 63 days of applying for the AARP program, pre-existing conditions may be waived. You must be between the ages of 50-64 to be eligible to apply for yourself and your dependents may be age 64 or under to apply for coverage.

Piggyback on your student's health plan

Some college student health plans allow unemployed parents to elect coverage during the open enrollment period. Or, in some cases, if the student is already enrolled, the parents can be added to the plan. Check with the college's financial aid office.

Pick up a part-time job

Many companies offer a healthcare benefits package to part-time employees. Typically, part-time workers have to pay a portion of the premium, but this may still be less costly than buying coverage on your own. These programs usually require that you work for the company for a specific amount of time and that you work a minimum number of hours a week before you become eligible for the plan.

Need personal help making a healthcare choice?

If you need help sorting through all of your healthcare options to find what is best for you and your family, contact an independent insurance broker. These brokers may represent numerous health insurance companies, and you don't have to pay them—the insurers do. A broker can help you find the best coverage for you, explain types of health insurance, and even help you resolve eligibility issues.

To find an independent broker near you, visit the **National Association of Health Underwriters** at **http://www.nahu.org**

Your membership association could save the day

Many college alumni and trade and professional associations offer group health coverage at a discounted rate.

Talk to your chamber of commerce about coverage

If your local chapter offers these benefits, you may be able to get health insurance on an individual basis—even if you do not have a business.

To find out more, call your local Chamber of Commerce or log on to its website.

Health Savings Accounts (HSAs)

If you enroll in a high-deductible health plan that meets government criteria for deductibles and coinsurance amounts, you may want to consider putting some money into an HSA to save for future healthcare costs. Contributions have annual limits, but you can deduct the contributions made to an HSA on your federal income taxes. Unreimbursed medical expenses can be paid with pre-tax dollars from your HSA.

For more information about HSAs,
visit the **U.S. Treasury Department**
at **http://www.treas.gov/offices/public-affairs/hsa**

For more information about health plans and a glossary of insurance terms, visit the government's

Agency for Healthcare Research and Quality
at **http://www.ahrq.gov/consumer/insuranceqa**

To link directly to health insurance companies, visit

America's Health Insurance Plans
at **http://www.ahip.org** or call **202-778-3200**

For more information on **AARP,**
visit **http://www.aarp.org/health/insurance**

FIND OUT
MORE
RESOURCES
TO USE

Little-Known
Cost-Cutting Strategies

Get doctor discounts, reduce hospital bills ... and more

Yes, it is possible to trim the costs of the care you receive from your doctors and other providers just by asking. Here's how to obtain low-cost or free services, without sacrificing quality.

Which doctors might forgo fees? Find out

The American Medical Association (AMA) or your state medical society may have a physician-referral service that can provide the names of doctors willing to forgo fees or accept a reduced fee for medical care.

To find a doctor in your area, visit the **AMA** at **http://webapps.ama-assn.org/doctorfinder/home.jsp**

Before a medical procedure, do your homework

Costs for medical procedures can vary greatly, depending on the facility where they are performed. The charge for a colonoscopy, for example, can range from a thousand dollars to twice that much, depending on where the procedure is done. You can call around to different hospitals and facilities to comparison-shop prices for procedures.

Health Advocate, the nation's leading independent healthcare and assistance company, offers employees Health Cost Estimator™, a valuable service that is used to compare the cost of common medical procedures within your area. For employees seeking more information, visit **http://www.HealthAdvocate.com**

Our consumer division, **Health Proponent®**, offers the same cost-comparison service. Visit: **http://www.HealthProponent.com**

Is a specialist always really necessary?

If you have a chronic condition such as asthma, diabetes, or arthritis, ask whether your primary doctor can take over your maintenance care. Generally, visits with primary care doctors, like family doctors, pediatricians, and general internists, are less costly than specialty care.

Participate in a clinical trial

Ask your doctor whether you qualify for a clinical trial. If so, you could reduce or eliminate the costs of your care—including medications.

To find a list of current clinical trials near you, visit the **U.S. National Institutes of Health** at **http://clinicaltrials.gov/ct2/search**

Check out a university dental clinic

University dental clinics are staffed by closely supervised dental students and interns, and, in some cases, you pay only for the cost of the materials you require. Contact your state dental society for the location of a dental school clinic in your area.

When you can't get in to see your doctor ...

For a non-life-threatening condition, such as a sprained ankle or a cold, consider using an urgent care or mini-clinic facility as an alternative when you can't get in to see your doctor. According to the National Women's Health Resource Center (**http://www.healthywomen.org**), visits to these facilities generally cost less than the ER, and the wait is shorter. If you have health insurance, check to see whether the center participates in your plan.

Ask your doctor for a discount

61 percent of adults surveyed who asked their doctor for a discount got one! Discuss a payment plan with your physician or hospital. To many doctors, even reduced payments are preferable to turning your bill over to a collection service. So ask!

Get low-cost—or free—mental health help

Here are a few options:

- **Mental health agencies.** Fees can be as low as $5 an hour. Call your county or state Department of Health to find agencies near you.

- **Reduced-fee group counseling**. Facilitated by local therapists.

- **Self-help groups.** Many meet for FREE to discuss shared issues.

- **Pastoral counselors.** Many are trained in mental health counseling and typically charge low rates. In some cases, fees are waived.

- **Teaching hospitals.** You may find lower-cost mental health care at teaching hospitals, where graduate-level students overseen by certified professionals provide services.

To find treatment or a support group near you, visit the **U.S. Substance Abuse and Mental Health Services Administration (SAMHSA) at http://www.samhsa.gov/treatment/index.aspx**

Do you have a debilitating disease? Here's help!

The Patient Advocate Foundation (PAF) provides professional case management services to Americans with chronic, life-threatening and debilitating illnesses. The foundation helps patients with issues from insurance appeals to patient education. Its PAF Co-Pay Relief program helps qualified patients who have chronic, life-threatening, and/or debilitating diseases with out-of-pocket costs.

For more information on the **Patient Advocate Foundation (PAF)**, visit **http://www.patientadvocate.org** or call **1-800-532-5274**

Free care at the drugstore:
an emerging trend

Lost your job? Eligible for federal or state unemployment benefits? Until the end of 2009, you can get free treatment for sinus infections, warts, and many other minor ailments at Walgreens' in-store Take Care Clinics. And this benefit is available to your spouse and dependent children from age 18 months to 18 years.

You must have used the clinic previously; otherwise, you'll pay the standard $59 clinic fee. Similar retail clinics, like the MinuteClinic facilities in many CVS drugstores, charge between $40 and $70 but may soon waive fees, too.

The retail clinics are staffed by nurse practitioners. These clinics do not replace the regular care you should receive from your doctor.

To find a **Walgreens Take Care Clinic** near you,
visit **http://www.takecarehealth.com/**

To find other retail-based clinics near you,
visit the **Convenient Care Association (CCA)**
at **http://www.ccaclinics.org** and select **"Looking for Clinics?"**

Remember to check for updates

Programs, websites, and phone numbers can continually change. We'll provide additional information and invite you to share important healthcare resources you've discovered too.

Go to **http://www.healthcaresurvivalguide.com**

Keep a Watch on Medical Bills

How to lower—or eliminate—doctor and hospital bills

When you're unemployed, it's important to carefully track your medical expenses. This is especially important when your care involves hospitalization, where bills can be sky-high. Here are ways to keep tabs on your bills and a lid on the costs of services.

Contact your insurer if you need to clarify coverage

If you are considering a medical service, call your insurer first to find out about coverage, preauthorization requirements, referrals, and what else you must do before you receive treatment. Be specific and keep records of whom you spoke with, and the date. This documentation can be used to dispute any incorrect information or claims issues.

Zero in on every doctor bill

Check your doctor receipts to verify the services billed. Compare it against the Explanation of Benefits (EOB) statement received from your insurance company.

Take charge: address errors

If you think there's been an error, for example, if your insurance company did not cover your annual physical or a preventive service as the plan stipulates—contact your insurer first. The bill can usually be easily reprocessed. You may find out that your insurance plan denied payment because your doctor's office made an error on their claim or the service you received was incorrectly coded. If so, ask the doctor's office to resubmit the claim using the correct codes. Then, talk with the insurance company to make sure the bill was correctly reprocessed.

To learn how to check your bill for errors, visit **http://familydoctor.org/online/famdocen/home/pat-advocacy/healthcare/888.html**

✔ What to do BEFORE you are hospitalized

☐ **Ask your doctor whether your care can be provided at a nonteaching hospital.**
Community hospitals are often less costly options than an academic medical center hospital. If your doctor does not have privileges at the community hospital, ask for a referral to another doctor who does.

☐ **Review your coverage.**
You may not realize that you can be billed for certain services not included on an emergency room bill, for example. If you have a "network" plan like an HMO or a PPO, make sure all providers treating you are covered.

☐ **Talk to the hospital *before* you get care.**
You may be able to negotiate payment for services.

☐ **Ask whether you can bring along your own medications.**
It may be a good way to avoid paying for the same drugs from the hospital pharmacy.

☐ **Keep track of the hospital care you receive.**
Enlist a friend or family member to help you keep track of all procedures, tests, medications, and supplies. This can help when you review your bills later.

☐ **Double-check your hospital bills.**
Duplicate billing, charging for an incorrect number of days in the hospital, and incorrect room charges are common errors. Bring any discrepancies to the attention of the hospital or your doctor as soon as possible.

Two more ways to cut hospital bills ...

Did you get charged for the wrong number of hospital days?

It's a common error. So look at your bill closely!

Pay cash, get a discount

If you pay cash for hospital services, you may be able to get a significant dollar or percentage discount. Many hospitals may also be willing to arrange a payment plan.

Look into hospital assistance programs—sometimes called charity care—for little or no cost.

How to dispute a claim or bill you have received

Here is the general sequence to address a claim:

1 **Gather your medical bills.** Include the Explanation of Benefits (EOB) notices and any correspondence from the parties involved in your case.

2 **Include complete notes.** List phone conversations you have had with anyone involved in your case. Include the date; the name of the person you spoke to and their phone number; the location of the call center; and the content of the conversation. This will add more credibility should you run into any problems later on.

3 **Discuss your dispute.** Call your doctor's office or your health plan.

4 **If necessary, file an appeal.** Call the customer service representative at your insurance plan to ask about the appeals process. Appeals instructions should also be specified in the EOB statement or denial letter you receive from your plan.

5 **Put your appeal in writing within the deadline.** Direct it to your insurer's claims processing or appeals department. Include a photocopy of the denial with your written appeal.

6 **Keep copies of all communication.**

If your appeal is denied ...

There are often several further options available to you if your appeal is denied. You can request a review by an outside independent review organization or even appeal to your state's insurance department. Some states have a health insurance ombudsman who helps consumers deal with insurance problems. Your health insurance plan is obligated to explain these additional appeal rights to you. If they don't, write letters to the Office of Consumer Affairs of your state's Attorney General's Office, the Department of Insurance, and the Department of Health. Include copies of your denial, your appeal, and any other written communication between you and your health insurance carrier.

Remember to check for updates

Programs, websites, and phone numbers can continually change.
We'll provide additional information and invite you to share important healthcare resources you've discovered too.

Go to **http://www.healthcaresurvivalguide.com**

For guidance on insurance claim disputes,
visit **http://unitedpolicyholders.org/claimtips.html**

To file a **Medicare** or **Medicaid** complaint,
visit **http://www.medicare.gov/basics/appeals.asp**

To view the U.S. **"Patients' Bill of Rights,"** visit the
National Institutes of Health at **http://www.cc.nih.gov/participate/patientinfo/legal/bill_of_rights.shtml**

FIND OUT
MORE
RESOURCES
TO USE

Best Ways to Get Drugs at a Discount (or Free!)

A dozen ways to lower—or erase—your cost

The average annual cost of a single prescription nearly doubled in a recent five-year period, according to research from the American Association of Retired Persons (AARP). Here is how to reduce—or eliminate—this expense.

Ask your doctor about nondrug strategies

Losing weight, eating a healthy diet, and quitting smoking may work as well as medication for your condition.

Get free samples

Getting free samples for a new medication from your doctor is a no-cost option. It especially makes sense if you don't need to continue the medication for long, or if your doctor changes your prescription.

Switch to generics

Ask your doctor whether you can take a generic equivalent that will be just as effective for any prescribed drug. A generic drug is likely to cost much less than its brand-name counterpart.

Shop around and scour websites

Generic drugs can range in cost from 20 to 80 percent less than brand-name drugs, depending on the pharmacy. For brand-name drugs, check websites of drug manufacturers for discount offers.

Look into retail discount drugs

Look into the discount generic prescriptions offered for as little as $4 by retailers such as Walmart, Target, and Kroger and members-only retailers such as Costco, Sam's Club, and BJ's Wholesale Club.

Can you substitute an OTC medication?

Ask your doctor whether you can substitute an over-the-counter (OTC) medication for your prescribed medication. One example: an OTC antihistamine substituted for a prescription sedative may work equally well and cost much less.

Get your prescriptions by mail

Ask your doctor to write a three-month prescription for your maintenance medications, such as insulin or a cholesterol-lowering medication. Many insurance plans allow a three-month supply at a discount or with lower co-pays when ordered through the mail-order program.

Check out volunteer- and community-based services

Many hospitals, universities, public organizations, charities, and advocacy groups have come together to form charitable partnerships to offer discount medications.

For more information about partnerships formed by community agencies such as the **American Cancer Society through the United Way,** visit **http://www.liveunited.org/health**

Look for free medications

A number of pharmaceutical companies offer limited-time only access to free prescription medications for those who qualify.

Here are a few examples:

Pfizer

This pharmaceutical manufacturer will provide those who lose their jobs with free prescriptions, beginning July 1, 2009, and lasting until December 31, 2009. To qualify, you must have been taking the Pfizer drug for at least three months. Watch to see whether other pharmaceutical companies provide similar offers.

To sign up or find out more about the 70 Pfizer prescriptions included in this limited-time offer, call toll-free **1-866-706-2400** or visit **http://www.PfizerHelpfulAnswers.com**

Johnson & Johnson, access2wellness

Access2wellness, sponsored by Johnson & Johnson, provides access to one of the broadest selections of pharmaceutical-company-sponsored medication assistance programs. The program is like a clearinghouse for programs that offer more than 1,000 prescription medications for free or at a discount to those who qualify.

To find out whether you qualify for a prescription assistance program call **1-866-317-2775**. or visit **http://www.access2wellness.com/a2w/index.html**

Dispense with high Rx costs

Get a free discount card

Many pharmacies and drug companies offer a free prescription card, available online, for discounts for both brand-name prescriptions and generics. You can print one out and hand it to the pharmacist.

To print out a Prescription Savings Card, available online, visit **http://www.PSCard.com**

You can also stop in at your local **United Way** office to get a free prescription drug discount card in partnership with **FamilyWize** or visit **http://www.familywize.com**

State Pharmaceutical Assistance Programs (SPAPs)

Depending on your state, you can get a discount on medications through an SPAP. Typically, there is no premium for these plans, but expect to pay a co-pay for your medications.

To find out about a **SPAP** in your state, visit the **U.S. Department of Health and Human Services** at **http://www.medicare.gov/spap.asp**

Remember to check for updates

Programs, websites, and phone numbers can continually change.
We'll provide additional information and invite you to share important healthcare
resources you've discovered too.

Go to **http://www.healthcaresurvivalguide.com**

Partnership for Prescription Assistance.
Including a list of links to all of the pharmaceutical
companies, as well as states that participate in the
programs: **http://www.pparx.org**

NeedyMeds.
http://www.needymeds.org/indices/needymedspage.shtml

RxAssist. **http://www.rxassist.org**

SPAP. http://www.medicare.gov/spap.asp

To compare drug prices within your zip code, visit **http://www.
consumerreports.org/health/best-buy-drugs/index.htm**

FIND OUT
MORE
RESOURCES
TO USE

Take Charge of Your Health
Get fit, ward off disease, live longer

Research shows that perhaps as many as three-fourths of diseases can be prevented by adopting healthy lifestyle habits. The impact of many chronic diseases can be reduced, which can mean fewer doctor visits and, possibly, a reduced need for medications. Even small changes can have a big impact on improving—and maintaining—health.

Put together a PHR

A personal health record (PHR) is a handy way to record and recall your medical history, past procedures, diagnoses, medications, allergies, etc. An online PHR can be printed out for your doctor to help provide updated information, avoid unnecessary tests, and help prevent mix-ups in diagnoses and medications.

You can find free, online PHRs from companies such as Google, Microsoft, and WebMD. Your health information is kept safe and private in compliance with government regulations.

For a free online PHR, visit Google Health **(http://www.google.com/ health)**, Microsoft's Health Vault **(http://www.healthvault.com)**, or WebMd **(http://www.webmd.com/phr)**

Engage in regular exercise

Just 30 to 60 minutes of exercise a day can reduce your risk for heart disease, high blood pressure, Type 2 diabetes, stroke, and certain types of cancer. (*Journal of the American Medical Association*, 2006)

Manage your stress

Stress-related factors are responsible for between 60 and 90 percent of doctor visits, Harvard researchers found. Engage in calm-inducing activities such as yoga, meditation, or exercise for at least 30 minutes each day.

Preventive screenings: keep them up

Screening and early detection can save lives. For example, an estimated 14,000 lives could be saved annually if 90 percent of adults over age 50 were up-to-date with screening for colorectal cancer, according to the National Commission on Prevention Priorities.

Before getting a preventive screening

Be sure to check with your insurer to see whether the specific screening will be covered. Insurers vary as to which preventive services they cover. In some cases, preventive services are offered free of charge, but it is important to verify this beforehand to avoid being billed.

The National Breast and Cervical Cancer Early Detection Program

This program offers women free and low-cost screenings for cervical and breast cancers. The American Cancer Society's research estimates that mammograms for women over the age of 40 at the recommended intervals could reduce breast cancer deaths by 63 percent.

For more information, visit **http://www.cdc.gov/cancer/nbccedp**

The Prostate Conditions Education Council (PCEC)

The council has a national screening program that offers any man, regardless of insurance circumstances, free prostate screenings. The screenings are available at health fairs, clinics, doctors' offices, and hospitals.

To find a free prostate screening near you, visit the **PCEC** at **http://www.prostateconditions.org/programs_and_events**

Screenings from the American Cancer Society (ACS)

The ACS can help you locate free or low-cost screenings for breast, prostate, and colon cancer in your area.

Call the **ACS** toll-free at **1-800-ACS-2345** or visit **http://www.cancer.org,** click on **"Find ACS in Your Community,"** and enter your zip code.

Perform self-exams

- **Regular breast self-exams and testicular self-exams** between screenings, combined with routine clinical exams, are vital.

- **Don't forget to scan your skin for irregular moles.**

Follow screening guidelines

- **Women should get mammograms yearly after age 40,** Pap tests yearly after age 18, and bone density tests at least once at age 65.

- **Men should have regular exams for prostate cancer,** beginning at age 40.

- **Both men and women should have a colonoscopy starting at age 50,** and have their cholesterol and blood glucose levels monitored regularly.

- **Men and women should get regular blood pressure checks starting at age 21.**

For guidelines on screenings, visit the **U.S. Preventive Services Task Force** at **http://www.ahrq.gov/clinic/uspstfix.htm#Recommendations**

Get free or low-cost screenings at health fairs

Many local health fairs offer free or low-cost screenings and important information. Check with your local health agencies, hospitals, and community centers to find a health fair in your area.

You can also visit **http://www.covertheuninsured.org** and click on **"Upcoming Events"** to find an upcoming health fair near you.

Planned Parenthood

Planned Parenthood provides low-cost reproductive health care services to both men and women, and includes screenings, annual exams, and prenatal care. Fees are based on what you can afford to pay.

To find out about a **Planned Parenthood** center near you, visit **http://www.plannedparenthood.org** or call toll-free **1-800-230-PLAN**

Be Proactive

Stop smoking

According to the Centers for Disease Control and Prevention (CDC), close to a half-million premature deaths occur as a result of smoking each year. The CDC also reports that nonsmokers exposed to secondhand smoke at home increase their risk of heart disease by 25–35 percent. Their lung cancer risk increases by 20–30 percent.

Smoking affects everyone

Secondhand cigarette smoke has higher concentrations of many cancer-causing and toxic chemicals than does smoke inhaled by smokers, according to the Surgeon General.

Drink alcohol in moderation

Excessive alcohol use, either in the form of heavy drinking or binge drinking, can lead to increased risk of health problems such as liver disease or unintentional injuries. The CDC recommends a limit of one drink per day for women and two drinks per day for men.

Improve your diet. Go gradual.

Eating plenty of nutritious and low-fat dairy products, fruits, vegetables, and whole grains, and substituting fish for red meat a few times a week can be very beneficial. Make changes gradually to help you adjust and adhere to a healthy diet. One suggestion: gradually switch from drinking high-fat to low-fat and then to skim milk stretched out over a few weeks.

Limiting salt intake to the recommended one teaspoon (about 2,300 mg—half of the typical intake) per day can lower your blood pressure by up to eight points, according to the American Heart Association. High blood pressure is a major factor of heart disease and a leading reason for doctor visits.

Lose weight

People who are overweight by 30 pounds can expect to pay $5,000 to $21,000 more in lifetime medical bills than their peers of normal weight. People who are 70 pounds or more above their ideal weight can incur lifetime medical expenses totaling $15,000 to $29,000 more than those of healthy weight, according to a 2008 study reported in the journal *Obesity*.

Keep a diary of what you eat

Keeping a food diary can help you double your weight loss. (*American Journal of Preventive Medicine*, 2004)

Lose just 5 percent of your body weight

You'll reduce your cholesterol and risk for heart disease, according to the National Institute of Diabetes and Digestive and Kidney Disease (NIDDK).

Practice good hygiene

Wash your hands! Prevent hand-to-hand infections

Wash your hands frequently or use an alcohol-based hand sanitizer to avoid the common cold, flu, and many causes of diarrhea.

Floss daily

Flossing helps to prevent tooth decay and periodontal disease. This gum condition often can lead to later periodontal surgery and can carry a price tag of anywhere from $4,000 to $10,000, as reported by the National Institutes of Health (NIH). And, according to the American Heart Association, maintaining good dental hygiene may reduce your risk of heart disease.

Discover Health Advocacy

Navigating the healthcare maze is not easy. You can get help.

Available healthcare information is often confusing and hard to figure out on your own. The idea behind health advocacy is that you have a knowledgeable person, usually someone experienced in the medical and/or benefits field, to help you find—and interpret—resources to make sound decisions about your healthcare.

You can get personal help to locate doctors and specialists and a full range of healthcare services. The advocate can provide real answers about cost-saving medication issues, clinical trials, and sources of affordable healthcare coverage.

Working on your behalf, health advocacy means that someone else can take on the task of interacting with your providers and insurance and handling thorny healthcare issues. You can receive clear explanations of health plan coverage and limitations and get one-on-one help to correct billing errors, negotiate provider fees, and address claims.

Health advocacy means that you have someone to guide you through the healthcare system and get you the resources you need, no matter what your income or insurance status.

Advocacy in Action

Real People. Real Stories. Real Results.

Nearly a decade ago, we built our company, Health Advocate, Inc., to help employees navigate the complex healthcare system and to provide them the answers they need when they need them most. Our core advocacy team of highly experienced medical experts and benefits and claims specialists has served millions of Americans, primarily through our thousands of employer relationships. With highly honed skills, extensive research capabilities, and compassion, our team has personally helped employees and their families resolve a full range of healthcare- and insurance-related issues. We've addressed untangling medical bills, negotiating provider fees, clarifying coverage, finding doctors, eldercare, support services, and more.

The consumer division of our service, Health Proponent, provides the same expert, personal assistance to help individuals resolve burdensome healthcare issues, saving them time, money, and worry.

Here are a few examples of how we have helped our members correct medical billing errors, find low-cost medications, locate eldercare, clarify coverage, and negotiate fees.

Real People. Real Stories. Real Results.

The following composite case studies illustrate how Health Advocate provided a healthcare lifeline when it was needed most.

Problem: Coverage for hospitalization

Elizabeth had been trying for more than a year to get her health insurance to cover the cost of a lengthy hospital stay as stipulated in her plan.

Solution: Health Advocate found a coding mistake and worked with Elizabeth's doctor, hospital, and health plan to correct it. Finally, all claims were processed for payment, saving Elizabeth $3,500.

Problem: Find eldercare

Karen needed help finding in-home care for her elderly mother, who wanted to remain living at home.

Solution: Health Advocate worked with Karen's local Office of Aging and located in-home care and an emergency call-button device for her mother. This allowed Karen to go to work without worry.

If you would like more information about health advocacy and how the consumer division of Health Advocate can help you and your family, call **Health Proponent**, toll-free, at **1-866-93-WE-HELP** or email us at **answers@HealthProponent.com**

Problem: Clarification of coverage, find support groups

Sally suffered a fractured hip resulting from osteoporosis, leaving her unable to stand for prolonged periods or to return to work. Her isolation worsened when her application for Supplemental Security Income (SSI), which would cover the cost of a walker, was held up.

Solution: Health Advocate helped facilitate Sally's application for coverage back to the onset of her disease. Our staff also located an appropriate support group to help Sally deal with the pain and difficulties she experienced with her mobility.

Problem: Lower-cost medication

Andrew's benefits did not cover the expensive drug he needed for a rare illness.

Solution: Health Advocate found an equally effective medication that Andrew's plan agreed to cover.

Problem: Comparing medical costs

Kelly's child needed tubes in her ears because of repeated ear infections. She wanted to compare costs for this procedure and also wanted an estimate of what she could expect to pay.

Solution: Health Advocate researched cost estimates for this procedure in her area; provided a detailed report listing low, likely, and high costs; and explained what her out-of-pocket costs were likely to be. This resulted in a potential savings of more than $7,000 dollars.

Talk to us. Let's keep the dialogue going!

Healthcare is continually changing and your feedback will help keep our information fresh. We'd love to hear from you. Give us a call or drop us a line if you have any questions. Tell us if the book is helpful to you and let us know your suggestions for updating our website.

 info@healthcaresurvivalguide.com

 1-866-969-3435

 http://www.healthcaresurvivalguide.com

You can follow us on Facebook and Twitter.